Things I like to do

By Kamto Nwabueze

THIS BOOK BELONG TO ....

I like to play outside, the sun is bright, the swing is fun, I like to play with my friend, we take turns.

I like to play with Legos, the pieces are big, I like to pile them high, I like to play with my cousin.

I like to play with clay, the colors
are pretty, I like to build dinosaurs,
I like to play with my friend.

CLAY
CLAY

I like to swim in the pool,
splashing is fun, the ball is round,
the water is warm.

I like to play with my dog in the park, my dog is fast, my dog is small, my dog is funny.

I like to watch tv during my play time, the shows are fun, I like shows with songs, I like to sing along with my favorite show.

I like to play games on my computer, my mommy helps me, there are so many games I like to play, the games are cool.

I like to read a book at bedtime, my dad reads to me, the room is quiet, the book is calm, it helps me fall asleep.